How Artists Use

PERSPECTIVE

Paul Flux

H **www.heinemann.co.uk**
Visit our website to find out more information about Heinemann Library books.

To order:

☎ Phone 44 (0) 1865 888066

▤ Send a fax to 44 (0) 1865 314091

▢ Visit the Heinemann Bookshop at www.heinemann.co.uk to browse our catalogue and order online.

First published in Great Britain by Heinemann Library, Halley Court, Jordan Hill, Oxford OX2 8EJ, a division of Reed Educational and Professional Publishing Ltd.
Heinemann is a registered trademark of Reed Educational and Professional Publishing Ltd.

OXFORD MELBOURNE AUCKLAND JOHANNESBURG BLANTYRE
GABORONE IBADAN PORTSMOUTH (NH) USA CHICAGO

Designed by Celia Floyd
Illustrations by Jo Brooker/Ann Miller
Originated by Ambassador Litho Ltd
Printed and bound by South China Printing in Hong Kong/China

ISBN 0 431 16202 6 (hardback)   ISBN 0 431 16207 7 (paperback)
06 05 04 03 02   06 05 04 03 02
10 9 8 7 6 5 4 3 2 1   10 9 8 7 6 5 4 3 2 1

British Library Cataloguing in Publication Data

Flux, Paul
    How artists use perspective. (Take-off!)
    1.Perspective – Juvenile literature
    I.Title
    701.8'2

Acknowledgements

The publishers would like to thank the following for permission to reproduce photographs:

AKG, London: Art Institute of Chicago pp6,7 Bern, Klee Foundation / DACS p21, National Gallery, London pp18, 19, Tate Gallery, London p17; Art Archive/ DACS: p16; Bridgeman Art Library: National Gallery, London pp4, 14, Private Collection p20; Ascending and Descending by M. C. Escher, c.2000 Cordon Art B.V.-Baarn-Holland. All rights reserved: p11; DACS: p26; National Gallery of Scotland, Edinburgh: p12; National Trust Photographic Library: Derrick E. Witty p13; 2000 The Museum of Modern Art, New York: pp24, 28; San Francisco Art Institute: David Wakely p9; SCALA: Collection Gianni Mattioli, Milan / DACS: p15; Städtisches Museum Abteiberg, Möchengladbach / DACS: p29; Yale University Art Gallery, New Haven, Connecticut: DACS p22.

Cover photograph reproduced with permission of Bridgeman Art Library/Musee d'Orsay.

Our thanks to Sue Graves and Hilda Reed for their advice and expertise in the preparation of this book.

Every effort has been made to contact copyright holders of any material reproduced in this book. Any omissions will be rectified in subsequent printings if notice is given to the publishers.

Contents

Any words appearing in the text in bold, **like this**, are explained in the Glossary.

What is perspective?

This painting is perfectly flat, yet it seems to have depth and height. **Perspective** is a way of showing space and distance in a picture. Here we can see far into the distance. Our eyes are drawn towards the window at the back.

Can you see the apple and marrow about to fall out of this picture?

Carlo Crivelli, *The Annunciation with Saint Emidius*, 1486.

No matter how often you look at this picture, the figure at the back will always seem to be the largest.

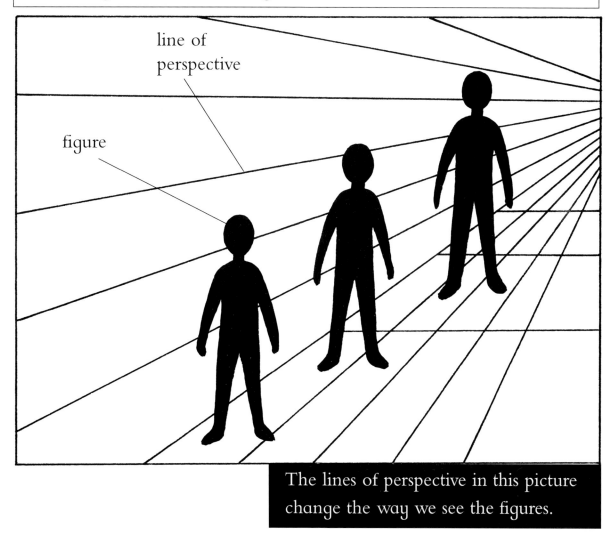

line of
perspective

figure

The lines of perspective in this picture change the way we see the figures.

Perspective changes the way we see things. Here you can see three simple figures, with lines of perspective disappearing towards the back of the picture. Try measuring the figures. The one at the front looks much smaller, but in fact all three are exactly the same size!

Lines of perspective

Gustave Caillebotte, *Paris Street, Rainy Day*, 1877.

This is Paris, France more than 100 years ago. You are walking towards two people who are not looking at you. Far into the distance everyone is going about their daily business. The artist has made you a visitor in a great city.

This painting is very large. In fact it is over 2 metres high and 3 metres wide, so the people in the front of the picture are just about life size!

vanishing point

line of perspective

The lines of perspective meet at the vanishing point.

The lines of **perspective** make us feel we are actually there in the painting. The place where the lines meet is called the **vanishing point**. Without perspective, this kind of picture would not work.

How the eye sees

Have you ever thought about how many different images you can see in a minute, and how many different messages go to your brain?

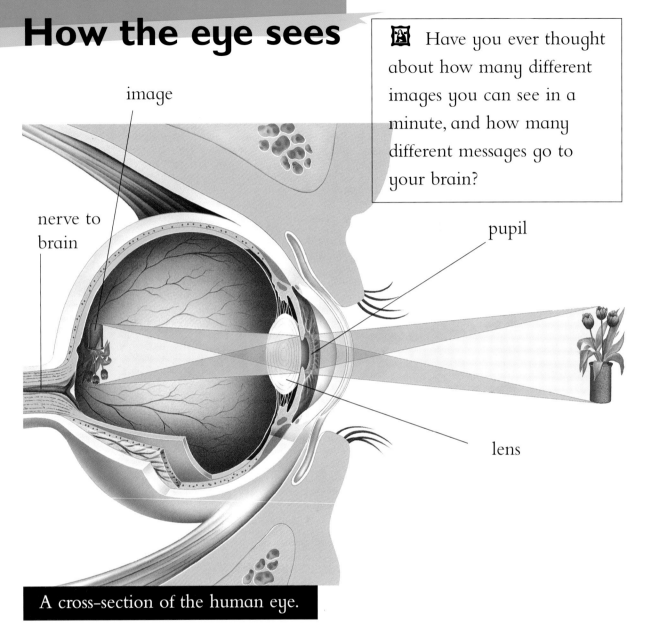

image

nerve to brain

pupil

lens

A cross-section of the human eye.

The human eye is very clever. The **image** of what we see passes through the lens and hits more than one hundred million **cells**. These cells send a message to the brain along **nerves**. All of this happens very quickly.

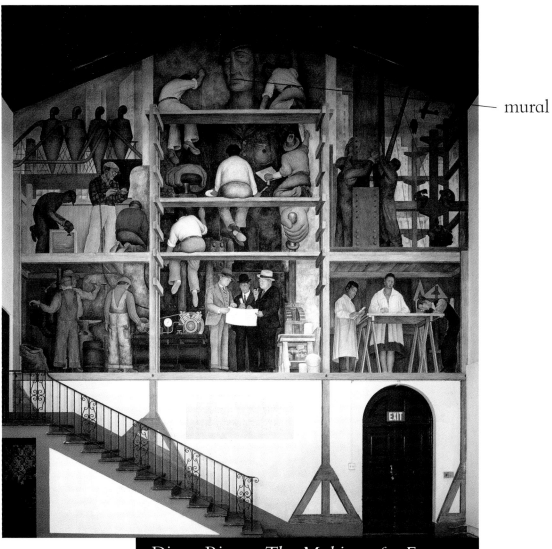

mural

Diego Rivera, *The Making of a Fresco Showing the Building of a City*, 1931.

Although our brain is very clever, it can be fooled by **perspective**. This picture is in two parts. One part shows the artist and his assistants painting a **mural**. The other part shows the mural.

9

Tricks of perspective

The word 'tri' means three. Why do you think this shape is called a tri-bar?

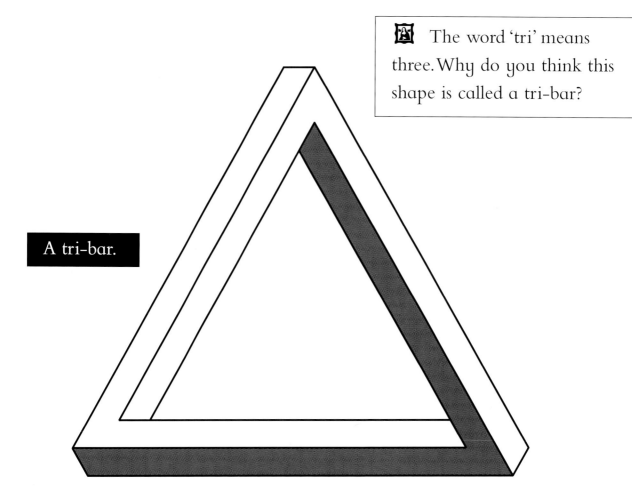

A tri-bar.

Perspective is a trick. It can fool the brain into believing something which cannot be true. This figure is called a tri-bar. Follow the lines with your finger and you will see that the shape is impossible. Your brain wants to see something which is real, and yet it knows that what it is seeing is impossible!

In this picture you can see people going up and down a staircase. Follow the figures round the staircase and you will find that they are going round endlessly. M. C. Escher has used perspective to trick the brain into seeing something which cannot be true.

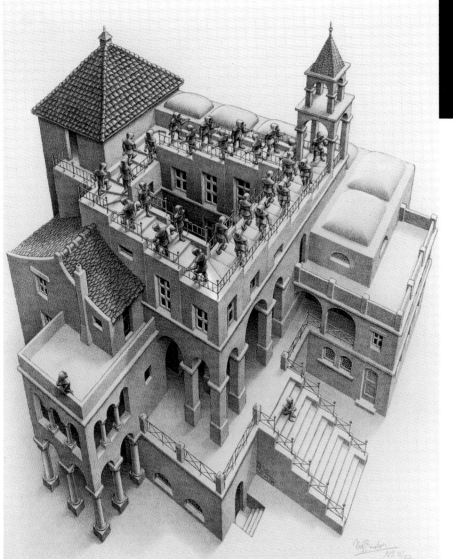

M. C. Escher, *Ascending and Descending*, 1960.

How artists make buildings look special

Look at the small people grouped together on the left of this picture. They give you some idea of how big this church is. The artist has used **perspective** to make it look much bigger than it is.

How long do you think it would take you to walk to the end of this church?

people

Pieter Saenredam, *Interior of St Bavo's Church*, 1648.

corridor

open door

Samuel van Hoogstraten, *A View Down a Corridor*, 1662.

Here you can see an open doorway in an old house, looking down a long corridor. But look again! The corridor doesn't really exist. It is just a painting in the doorway!

Seeing into the distance

The buildings disappear into the background. Can you find the **vanishing point** in this picture? Look on page 7 to see how.

Antonio Canaletto, *The Basin of San Marco on Ascension Day*, about 1740.

Canaletto painted this picture of Venice on one of the most important days of the year. The ruler of Venice is about to throw a ring into the water, to bless all the ships that travel in and out of the city.

Objects should get narrower as they go away from us — but what do you notice about the box in this picture?

Giorgio de Chirico, *Disquieting Muses*, 1916.

In this painting you can see a wooden stage with statues and tall buildings in the distance. A strange green light and deep shadows cover a mysterious building. Our eyes look past the central figures to the back of the picture.

15

Perspective, light and colour

Perspective and colour can be used to create the feeling of open space. In this painting, smoke makes it hard to see far. But we know that it is a railway station and that the railway lines will stretch off into the distance.

Claude Monet, *La Gare St-Lazare*, 1877.

Here is another early railway **scene**. This time we are out in the open, standing in the centre as a train rushes towards us. The far distance is lost in mist. The space is huge. Even the train seems small here.

Can you find the tiny boat in this painting? It looks lost in the mist and the rain.

bridge

steam train

William Turner, *Rain, Steam and Speed*, about 1844.

Bringing things up close

Paolo Uccello, *The Battle of San Romano*, 1450-60.

soldier
lying down

This painting by Uccello does not work very well because there is no single **vanishing point**. But parts of the painting are brilliant! It is very difficult to draw a person lying down from one end, but look at the soldier at the front on the left.

Uccello was one of the first artists to study **perspective**. He lived from 1397 to 1475.

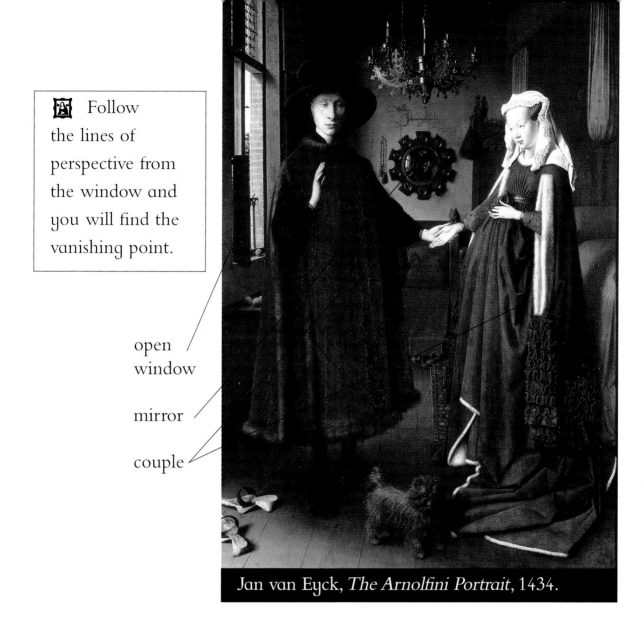

Follow the lines of perspective from the window and you will find the vanishing point.

open window

mirror

couple

Jan van Eyck, *The Arnolfini Portrait*, 1434.

This is a much better use of **perspective**. The room drifts away from us and the mirror reflects the **scene** back. We are watching an important moment. It could even be a marriage. The open window reminds us that the real world is just outside.

19

Changing views of perspective

Around 100 years ago some artists began to **experiment** with **perspective**. They painted parts of objects from different **angles** in the same picture, like this painting of a **mandolin**.

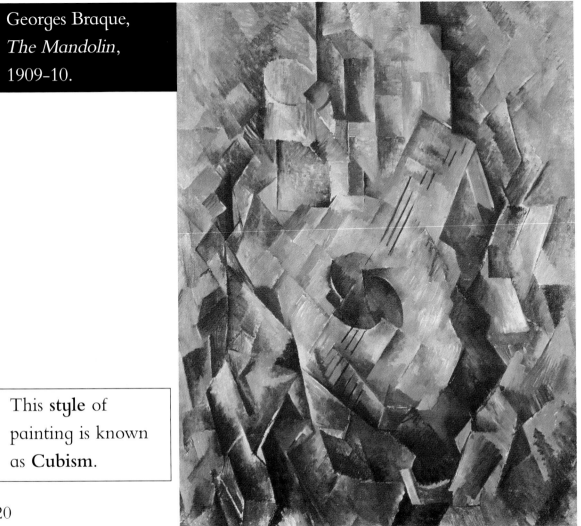

Georges Braque,
The Mandolin,
1909–10.

This **style** of painting is known as **Cubism**.

Paul Klee was a Swiss painter and a **graphic artist**. He lived from 1879 to 1940.

Some artists do not use perspective. Paul Klee has used **images** of things he has seen in the park and mixed them together. Images of people playing games, trees, flowers and open spaces make a **decorative panel**, full of life and colour.

21

How to use perspective

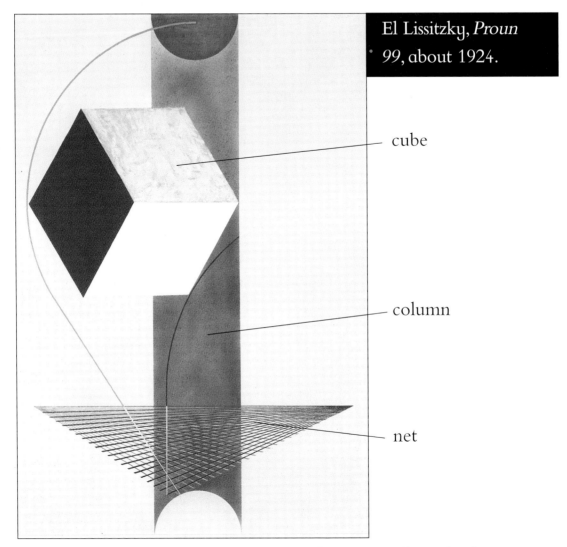

El Lissitzky, *Proun 99*, about 1924.

cube

column

net

The Russian artist El Lissitzky **experimented** with shapes and patterns. Here a cube seems to float in space, while a net moves away into the distance. The central column looks very flat. The simple shapes and sharp lines of the picture make it look like an **architect's** drawing.

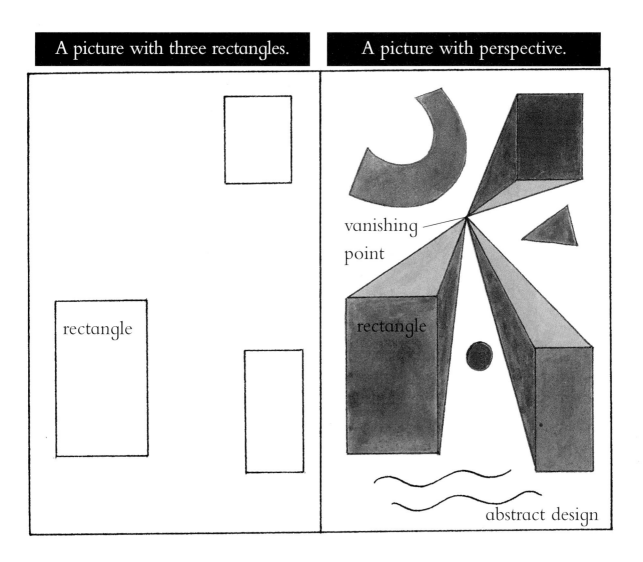

A picture with three rectangles.

rectangle

A picture with perspective.

vanishing point

rectangle

abstract design

Try drawing a picture with **perspective**:

1. Draw rectangles of different sizes on a sheet of paper.
2. Join three corners of each rectangle to a **vanishing point**.
3. Colour in the shapes.
4. Add some flat **abstract** designs to make your picture more interesting.

How to paint a landscape

Here a modern artist has used **perspective** to create a dramatic landscape. You can almost feel yourself travelling fast along the road. The steep lines of perspective give the flat surface a feeling of great depth.

Allan D'Arcangelo, *US Highway 1, Number 5*, 1962.

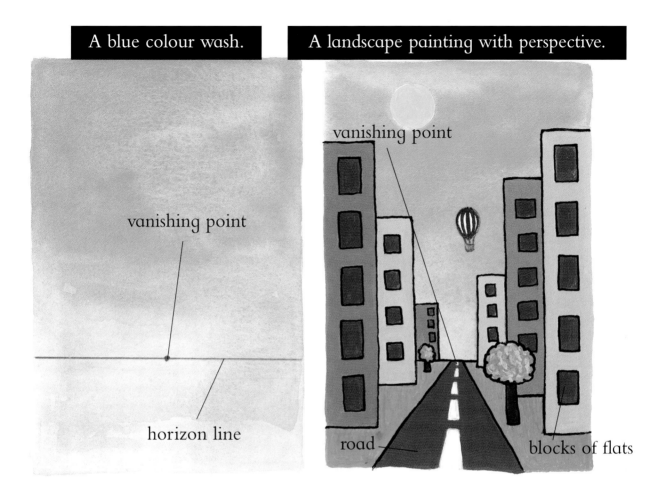

A blue colour wash.

A landscape painting with perspective.

vanishing point

horizon line

vanishing point

road

blocks of flats

Try painting a landscape with perspective:

1. Cover a large sheet of paper with a light blue **colour wash**. Mix in a little white to change the **shade** of the sky.
2. Draw the **horizon** line low on the paper and put the **vanishing point** in the centre.
3. Draw blocks of flats. Put the tallest at the sides of the painting and make them smaller as you near the vanishing point.
4. Finish off your picture with trees. Perhaps you could add an alien spaceship!

Figures in perspective

Victor Vasarely, *Study of Perspective*, 1935.

Look at this picture and the one on page 5. Here the
vanishing point is in the centre of the white rectangle.
The artist has drawn in the lines of **perspective** to make
a tunnel. He has drawn three figures coming towards us.

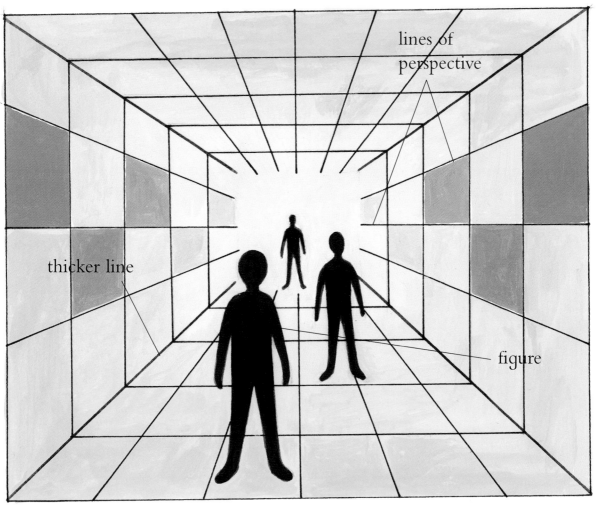

lines of
perspective

thicker line

figure

Now try drawing some figures in perspective:

1. Draw a square or rectangle near the centre of a piece of paper.
2. Next put in the lines of perspective as shown in the picture above.
3. Draw the four lines of from the corners a bit thicker.
4. Now draw three figures in different sizes. Put the larger figures near the bottom of the page.
5. Colour some of the spaces. Make the colours lighter at the back. It will look as if light is coming from the middle of the picture.

Making the ordinary different

Edward Hopper, *Gas*, 1940.

In this picture Edward Hopper uses **perspective** in a very clever way. Look carefully at the three petrol pumps. In real life they would all be about the same size, but the rules of perspective say that things further away from us should be smaller. The front pump is nearly twice the size of the back one.

Andy Warhol, *Campbell's Soup Can*, 1962.

Andy Warhol painted these everyday objects in 1962. The smaller can seems further away because of its size. You can do the same with an object of your own. Choose something which you can draw quite easily. A jug or cup would be fine. Make three drawings in different sizes, putting the smallest in the middle.

Glossary

a
b
c
d
e
f
g
h
i
j
k
l
m
n
o
p
q
r
s
t
u
v
w
x
y
z

abstract — kind of art which does not try to show people or things, but instead uses shape and colour to make the picture

angle — space between two straight lines which meet at a single point, or a viewpoint

architect — person who designs buildings

canvas — strong woven material on which many artists paint

cell — small, simple building block of any living thing

colour wash — layer of thin paint which covers a wide area of a picture, usually applied with a large brush

Cubism — way of painting, developed by Picasso and Braque, in which objects are shown from different angles in the same picture

decorative panel — part of a picture, wall or piece of furniture which has been painted to make it more interesting to look at

experiment — try things out or repeat something until you like the result

graphic artist — artist who designs, paints and draws

horizon — line at which the earth and sky seem to meet

illusion — something which is not real

image — likeness of a figure or object

landscape	picture of natural and man-made scenery, like fields, trees and houses
mandolin	kind of musical instrument
mural	picture or decoration painted onto a wall
nerve	very thin cords along which information goes around the body
perspective	way an artist draws or paints on a flat surface, so that there seems to be space and distance in the picture
scene	landscape or view painted by an artist
shade	darker or lighter version of a colour
skill	ability to do something difficult really well
style	the way in which a picture is painted
trompe-l'oeil	French for 'tricks the eye' – kind of painting in which the eyes are tricked into seeing something as real while, in fact, it is painted on a flat surface
vanishing point	place in a picture where all the lines of perspective meet and where the picture seems to disappear into the distance. Some pictures may have more than one vanishing point.

Index